The Menace of the Money-Power

An Analysis of World Government by Finance

by

A.K. Chesterton

The A.K. Chesterton Trust

2012

This booklet was first printed in 1946.

This edition is *The A.K. Chesterton Trust* Reprint Series No. 4.

Printed & Published 2012.

ISBN 978-0-9564669-3-8

© The A.K. Chesterton Trust, BM Candour, London, WC1N 3XX, United Kingdom.

Website: www.candour.org.uk

<u>**Foreword**</u>

This booklet was first published just after World War Two. Our new edition illustrates the fact that financial turmoil is nothing new, and that such events can be created to serve the interests of some.

When Chesterton completed his work, the Russian bear was beginning to make its presence felt as a rival to The Money Power, while a weakened and shackled Great Britain was just beginning the process of having its Empire – its World Heritage – torn from it.

66 years later the world is gripped by financial chaos. The British Empire and Russian Communism are long gone. It is to be hoped that The Money-Power has overstepped itself and has been dealt a serious blow, but history must be the judge of that.

We shall see.

Colin Todd

The A.K. Chesterton Trust
August 2012

<u>Preface</u>

The final deductions in this treatise, and in particular the relating of the Final Act of Bretton Woods to the financial policy which led to the foundation and perversion of the U.S. Federal Reserve Board, are the author's own, for which he must not fasten any responsibility upon his authorities.

 Those readers, however, who wish to check the facts from which the deductions are made may be recommended to the following works: "*All These Things*" and "*The Truths About The Slump*" by A. N. Field; "*The Bankers' Conspiracy*" and "*A Fraudulent Standard,*" by Arthur Kitson; "*Analysis of Usury*" and "*The Modern Idolatory,*" by Jeffrey Mark; "*The Mystical Body of Christ and the Reorganisation of Society,*" by Father Denis Fahey ; "*The Money Illusion,*" by Professor Irving Fisher; "*The Two Nations*" and "*The Breakdown of Money,*" by Christopher Hollis; "*Post-War Monetary Stabilisation,*" by Professor Gustav Cassel; "*America Conquers Britain,*" by Ludwell Denny; "*The Brief for the Prosecution,*" by Major C. H. Douglas; and the volumes of *Hansard* covering the debate on the Loan Agreement.

Another book, "*The Economics of Human Happiness,*" by W. Collin Brooks, although it draws none of the conclusions here set down, and indeed draws some which are at variance with them, is nevertheless well worth reading because of the wonderful lucidity with which its author deals with perversions of the monetary system.

A.K. Chesterton

THE MENACE OF THE MONEY POWER

MONEY can only be understood in terms of power. In the hands of the consumer it is power over goods. In the hands of the creative capitalist it is power over the means to produce goods. In the hands of the finance-capitalist, or money-lender, it is not only power over producers and consumers, but power as well over nations and their governments.

The technique of money-lending on its simplest level is to make an advance against security, draw interest, and at an agreed date receive back the capital sum—other things being equal, a perfectly honest transaction. If the more ambitious money-lenders kept to this even routine, however, they would be a very long time attaining power. What they desire, therefore, is that the money they lend shall either be repaid to them when its buying power has been greatly enhanced, or that it shall not be repaid at all, thus enabling them to foreclose on their mortgages and become possessed of their victim's capital assets. These two *motifs* have long determined the course of economic history, explaining slump and boom, and enabling a small band of international lenders and manipulators to become the virtual masters of the world. The method was explained, with almost incredible candour, in an article which appeared in *The U.S.A. Bankers Magazine*[1] on August 26th, 1934:

"Bonds and mortgages must be foreclosed as rapidly as possible. When through a process of the law the common people lose their homes they will become more docile and more easily governed through the strong arm of government applied by a central power of wealth under the control of leading financiers. This truth is well known among our principal men now engaged in forming an

imperialism of capital to govern the world. By dividing voters by the political party system we can get them to expend their energies in fighting over questions of no importance. Thus by discreet action we can secure for ourselves what has been so well planned.'"

Before investigating how this amiable programme has been, and is being, fulfilled, one popular fallacy should at once be exploded—the fallacy that this "imperialism of capital" has been set up in the teeth of Left-Wing opposition. The contrary is true.

Revolution throughout has been the friend and ally of finance-capitalism. Whether or not the French Revolution increased the sum of human liberty, equality and fraternity offers a subject for debate, but there can scarcely be any debate about its one concrete fact, which was the sweeping away of the Monarchial State and the founding in place thereof of the Bankers' State. The Revolution of 1848 brought precious little happiness to ordinary human beings, but out of it arose the central banking system of Germany, which reached its apotheosis under the Weimar Republic, when financiers achieved more absolute power than they had ever before enjoyed. The Russian Revolution, which furnishes a complete picture of the inter-relation between international capitalism and socialism, will be considered later. Some account must first be given of the way finance works.

If a group of men in any country wishes to secure financial control over that country's destinies, the most obvious initial step is to gain control of the issue of currency. This involves two cardinal principles—a single, controllable currency basis, such as gold, and a monopoly of the right to circulate notes and otherwise issue credit on that foundation. The banking history of the United States shows how the manipulators went to work to attain these objectives. Their weapon in every case was a deliberately engineered Stock Exchange panic, bringing ruin upon thousands of honest producers.

In 1890 there was in America a monetary stringency, to counteract which the Government three years later introduced the Sherman Silver Purchase Act, providing the means, by Government purchases of silver, of preventing currency contraction. The financiers moved swiftly into battle. This threat to gold, their chosen medium, could not be tolerated. The American Banking Association circulated to members instructions to sabotage the Government's plan:—

"Silver, silver certificates and treasury notes must be retired," ran its fiat, "and national bank notes upon a gold basis made the only money. This will require the authorisation of 500 millions to 1,000 millions of new bonds as the basis of circulation. You will at once retire one-third of your circulation and call in one half of your loans. Be careful to make a monetary stringency among your patrons, especially among influential business men. Advocate an extra session of Congress to repeal the purchasing clause of the Sherman Law."[2]

Even at that time finance enjoyed a measure of international power, for India was brought in to help the campaign, which she did by stopping the minting of silver. This, in conjunction with the panic deliberately induced by the New York bankers, caused the closing-down of silver mines, the shutting of factories, the crashing of banks, widespread ruin—and, of course, the repeal of the offending Act. Gold henceforward was to be the sole basis of currency, as the bankers had planned.

While crashes of this diabolical kind had often, as here, a political motive, it is to be noted that those at the heart of the conspiracy invariably managed to turn the chaos to their own immense financial advantage. One direct result of the 1893 panic was the transference of the Union Pacific Railroad into the hands of Jacob Schiff, head of the banking firm of Kuhn, Loeb and Company—to-day the monarchs of international finance. A few years later, moreover, Schiff managed to bring the mighty Great Northern Pacific Railway crashing to the ground, and from the ensuing panic his firm emerged as the complete masters of American railway finance: through Northern Securities Company it controlled £264,200,000 worth of stock and became an acknowledged member of the Money Trust which dominated the entire field of American Capitalism.

Jacob Schiff was now to be joined in Kuhn, Loeb and Company by Paul Warburg, scion of one of the great German banking families, and together they moved forward to the attainment of the second objective—control of all currency through a central banking system. In 1907 there was another great crisis when the Knickerbocker Trust failed, not because of any general panic action by the ordinary investor, but because manipulators of the millionaire class wilfully created a run on the banks. From this debacle they emerged incomparably more powerful, having bought up the stock of the ruined victims, which they held to re-sell at par. At the same time the Steel Trust was able to complete its absolute monopoly.

It may or may not have been a coincidence that Solomon Loeb, of Kuhn, Loeb and Company, was a member of Knickerbocker Trust. At any rate, the attainment of a central banking system was brought very much nearer to fulfilment—that consummation so devoutly wished by Kuhn, Loeb and Company.

Appalled at the ducks and drakes which were being played with the money-system, many genuine idealists in the United States— chief among them Woodrow Wilson and William Jennings Bryan, that doughty foe of the Money-Power—determined upon large-scale reforms to create order in place of the prevailing brigandage. And it so happened that there was a gentleman at hand only too happy to help them. His name was Mr. Paul Warburg! What did they want? To secure stability in the price level? Why, Mr. Warburg had the precise specific up his sleeve—a Federal Reserve System which would hold reserves centrally and despatch supplies of credit at once to any necessitous bank in the system that might call for them.

His plan, in most essentials, was the one adopted, and on December 20th, 1913, Mr. Carter Glass, sincerely denouncing the old laissez-faire order, secured the passage through the House of Representatives of the Federal Reserve Act, the vital clause of which, when the Bill was introduced, was a provision for the fixing of the discount rate to promote stability in the price level. How ironical was it, therefore, that when the Bill emerged these words "to promote stability in the price level" were surreptitiously dropped! At subsequent investigations officials of the Federal Reserve Board even denied that such had ever been its function. Two years later, Sir Cecil Spring-Rice, our Ambassador to the United States, placed on record the fact that the group of financiers associated with Kuhn, Loeb and Company had become supreme in America, and that Paul Warburg *was* the Federal Reserve Board!

William Jennings Bryan lived long enough to stand aghast at the horrified thought of what his name, in all innocence, had helped to bring into being, but no such shame cast a shadow on the happiness of Warburg and his friends, who now had exclusive power of note issue to the reserve banks, as well as power to fix the discount rate, which meant, of course, power to determine the amount of money in existence. They had conquered America: they were now ready to conquer the world.

It has been suggested that revolution is a good friend to the finance-capitalists, but they have an even better friend—war. War makes them the dictators of mankind. How lucky for them that, the year following the setting up of the Federal Reserve Board, a war should duly have arrived to complete their happiness!

War has several advantages. It places the nations engaged therein in urgent need of credits, which the financiers can bestow on their own terms. It unsettles things, making it easier to change the masters of a people. And in this particular war it seemed likely that many kings would lose their thrones—a pleasurable thought for those who opposed to the Monarchial State the larger beatitude of the Bankers' State. In particular, and for motives which need not be investigated in this strictly non-racial treatise, the Kuhn, Loeb bankers had their eye on one monarch whose head above all others they wished to see rolled in the sand—the head of the Czar of all the Russias. That is one reason why, in 1914, they were so ardently pro-German and so hostile to Britain. The Bolshevik Revolution of 1917 changed all that. Simple people imagine that the Russian Revolution was a protest against just such a system of wicked financial manipulation as I have described. What would be their surprise if they knew that the Bolsheviks were directly subsidized by—can they guess?—Messrs. Schiff, Paul Warburg, Max Warburg and the entire Kuhn, Loeb and Company outfit!

The first war objective, therefore, was gained when Imperial Russia fell. There was no longer the same reason for hating Britain, especially as Britain had done that which arouses love in the hearts of all true money-lenders--got hopelessly and inextricably into their debt. The late Lord Reading negotiated with the United States a loan of £1,000,000,000 which that optimistic gentleman promised that we should repay on demand—and in *gold*!

Thereafter there was no need for the Schiffs and the Warburgs to worry about Britain: we were safely in the bag. And if the war ended with the defeat of Germany and Austria—well, that would be at least two more crowned heads out of the way of a bankers' world state. America duly entered the war on our side!

First fruits of the great victory, for the Wall Street financiers, was the extension of their power to Britain and the Dominions, forcing us to surrender our command of the seas, to break our alliance with Japan, and, in a very short time, to return to the gold-standard, after which their associated concerns, such as General Electric, began to acquire our capital assets. They penetrated into every part of Europe and Africa. In China they became supreme in the international financial consortium which was formed to exploit that country. They were active in India. They conquered all South America except the Argentine. And in the United States itself they went from strength to strength by using the mechanism of the Federal Reserve Board for purposes diametrically the opposite from that for which it had supposedly been formed: that is, instead of forwarding supplies of credit when necessary to avoid a panic, they used the opportunity again and again to cut off credit supplies altogether.

By such means, in the early twenties, they encouraged the farmers under boom conditions to borrow and expand their enterprises, and then promptly called in the loans, delivering thousands into bankruptcy. Precisely the same technique caused the panic of 1929 which led to the great crash of 1931. Orthodox economists attribute this later disaster to the failure of the Creditanstalt in Vienna, arguing that it set in motion the whole succession of breakdowns which followed throughout the world. That, however, is a very incomplete picture of the actual situation. Mr. Louis T. McFadden, Chairman of the U.S. House of Representatives Banking and Currency Committee, referring to the New York Stock Exchange Collapse which began the American end of the slump, declared:

"It was not accidental. It was a carefully contrived occurrence ... the international bankers sought to bring about a condition of despair here so that they might emerge as the rulers of us all."

Nothing could be less equivocal than that. What cannot be denied is that in 1928 the Federal Reserve Board was feverishly expanding credit to create a boom, and next year as feverishly restricting credit to create a slump.

Major C. H. Douglas, in his brilliantly penetrating book, "*The Brief for the Prosecution*," asserts that the motive of the financiers was to crush the many industrialists who, because of prosperous times, had begun to "muscle-in" on the money-lending racket. This is not to argue, of course, that the crisis in the German banking system did not deepen and broaden the slump: the defaulting on reparations in 1931 led directly to the London crash. But even here a decisive part had been played by the Wall Street manipulators.

Throughout the evil Weimar regime in Germany, the American group, in collaboration with their associates in Germany, had been conducting a colossal fraud at the expense of the American people. Worthless German script and much of very little worth were freely accepted, largely through the instrumentality of Paul Warburg, as security for towering cash advances—computed by Mr. McFadden as over 30,000,000,000 dollars beyond the value of all the German bonds and these advances were poured into Germany (some, through Germany into "anti-capitalist" Russia) to make for international usury the most joyous gala period of its long and unsavoury history.

The game could not last: what is more, its perpetrators knew that it could not last, and had persuaded President Hoover in 1931 to stand by with a moratorium to tide their friends in Germany over the worst of their difficulties. Mr. McFadden, speaking of the moratorium, said: "If the German international financiers of Wall Street had not had this job waiting to be done, Herbert Hoover would never have been elected President of the United States." Describing the agency by which the business had been engineered, he told Congress:

"We have in this country one of the most corrupt institutions the world has ever known. I refer to the Federal Reserve Board and Federal Reserve Banks. This evil institution has impoverished and ruined the people of the United States. . . They have been peddling the credit of this Government and the signature of this Government to the

swindlers and speculators of all nations. This is what happens when a country forsakes its constitution and gives its sovereignty over public currency to private interests. Give them the flag and they will sell it."

This time, however, the Federal Reserve Board group had over-reached itself. Although the result of the world-wide crashes had been to strengthen the power of the big combines everywhere, and greatly to increase bank holdings of industrial stock, the slump nevertheless went too far; much further than it was intended to go.

Two signal events proclaimed this fact. First, Great Britain, in a desperate attempt to extricate herself, was forced off gold (as were thirty-four other nations!) and obliged to insulate her economy within a sterling area and a system of Imperial Preference. Repeated attempts have been made by the dollar-manipulators to crash the sterling area: only now are they about to succeed. To this mild but not incompetent British insurrection was added a much more terrifying phenomenon. Out of a Germany devastated by the Money-Power arose—Adolf Hitler. Hitler's revolt was not mild. It challenged the entire concept of international lending and established as the basis of trade the mutual exchange of goods, without recourse to the usurers.

There had been pioneers before Hitler. Kemal Ataturk had carried through the reconstruction of Turkey without borrowing a penny from abroad. Mussolini had safeguarded Italian currency against foreign speculators and striven as far as possible to build up for his people a self-contained economy. He was to have successors in Spain and Portugal. After the emergence of Hitler, however, it became clear that the international financial system was in mortal danger and that only by another war could it ever regain control over its vast empire—the empire built and maintained by debt. As it happened, Hitler was only too happy to oblige, and war came.

War would have come in any case. As Joseph Stalin has put on record:

"It would be incorrect to think that the war arose accidentally or as the result of the fault of some of the statesmen. Although those faults did exist, the war arose in reality as the inevitable result of the development of the world economic and political forces on the basis of monopoly capitalism."

The master-financiers of America, and their associates elsewhere, breathed again: now they would be able, not only to retrieve all the ground they had lost, but, by careful planning, to ensure that such rebellions never again occurred, or—if they did occur—that they should be put down by international armed force. As in 1913, they had grafted their wicked designs upon President Wilson's idealism to secure their precious central banking system, so in 1919 they had done precisely the same thing to secure that "hope of all the ages," the League of Nations.

One of the first actions of the League was to recommend all member states to return to the gold-standard, which leaves little room for doubt, even if no other evidence were available, that it was from the beginning the kept creature of the Money-Power. Geneva, however, was a sad disappointment to its promoters. When the opportunity came to coerce the rebel nations, "not a ship, not a gun," was available for the job. Next time the chosen instrument should have "teeth to enforce the Wall Street writ. This was decided long before the war came to an end—at Dumbarton Oaks. The war was to fulfil everything else that had been expected of it.

The first rebel to be brought to heel was Great Britain, whose foreign assets were taken over by New York almost *en bloc*, and who was for the most part forbidden to export, so that her foreign markets might be captured by the United States. Thereafter, as we shall see presently, much more ambitious plans were prepared to ensure her complete subjection to Wall Street. The last rebel to be vanquished—for in this sense Japan did not come within the rebel class—was Germany.

Germany's fate does not need to be described: the one consoling feature of her plight is that she brought it upon herself by virtue of her warrior-dream, which the masters of the world were able so relentlessly to use against her for her own destruction.

Britain restored to the comity of international finance, all rebels on the other side shattered, an international organisation, with "teeth," formed to keep the Money-Lenders' Peace—these be rich gains for Wall Street, but they are not the only gains.

We have seen how Paul Warburg managed to foist his idea of a central banking system on Woodrow Wilson and other sincere reformers. He represented it as a device for securing stability in the price level, but as soon as it was set up he used it to maintain instability of prices, a condition essential for the practise of large-scale usury. Within two years, as our Ambassador in Washington reported, he and his friends had become the financial masters of America. If it were possible to go further, and establish the same device on an international scale, would it not enable the world's strongest national reserve banking system to control its activities, so that the controllers of the national system could become the financial masters of the whole world?

The successors of Schiff and Warburg on the Federal Reserve Board evidently asked themselves this question and answered with an emphatic "Yes."

While the Second World War had still a long way to go to its determined end, "experts" suddenly began, both here and in America, to prepare plans for a "sound" monetary policy after it was over. Then came a gathering at a sylvan spot called Bretton Woods. By this time the reader will scarcely require to be told that its avowed object was to secure stability in the price level!

There was one other similarity to the campaign for the passing of the Federal Reserve Act. This Act was preceded by the Aldrich Bill, a more extreme measure which failed to get through the House of Representatives. So was the Final Act of Bretton Woods preceded by the more drastic White Plan. It would almost seem in each case that the extreme measure was put first, to make the succeeding compromise seem the more gracious. However that might be, the Final Act of Bretton Woods was duly presented to the nations for approval.

Lord Keynes arrived back in this country to commend it with great eagerness. It would, he assured us, secure stability of prices. The mechanism which it proposed to set up would conduct funds lying idle to irrigate the currency of any necessitous area which might need them. In precisely this kind of language did Woodrow Wilson commend the Federal Reserve Board system. We know now that the Federal Reserve system, instead of doing what Wilson had intended, often deliberately withheld credit where it was needed in order to create a panic. We know, too, that it enabled the strongest group within its complex of interests to gain control of its policy and of the economic policies of the American nation. Few things are more astonishing in economic history than the apparent failure of the late Lord Keynes to lay the moral to his heart.

The first objective of Bretton Woods is, of course, the linking of all currencies to gold. When sterling is fixed in terms of gold it will not be allowed to fluctuate above one per cent. There will be an obligation to buy and sell gold at a fixed buying and selling price. Member nations, moreover, will be obliged to include gold, in a given ratio, in their quotas to the International Monetary Fund, as well as in their contributions to the International Bank—the lodging of security against loans that have still to be advanced! The New York bankers have thus won on a world-scale the battle which they won on a national scale in 1893: Henceforward gold is to be the measure of things. And they control the gold!

Potentially even more catastrophic is the provision that nations will be unable, without the express consent of the Lords of Gold, to devalue their currencies above ten per cent. The seriousness of this enactment can only be understood by recalling that when, in 1931, it was vital for Britain to sever the link which bound her to the evil New York system, she found it necessary to devalue up to 27 per cent. Wall Street is determined that such a thing shall not be allowed to happen again. Should Britain or any other hard-pressed country attempt an unauthorized devaluation the international bankers will possess means of securing immediate redress.

What means? The answer takes one's breath away by virtue of its truly monumental impudence. Power has been vested in gentlemen of the kidney of the late Paul Warburg to declare the defaulter an outlaw among nations. They can order member States not to trade with her, and so starve her people into submission. If Britain were to default, her own Dominions, on pain of dire penalties, would be required to employ economic sanctions against her: similarly if a Dominion defaulted the Mother Country would be called upon—as *Truth* forcefully pointed out —to "repay the blood-loyalty and sacrifices of two wars by declaring an economic war on that Dominion." Could anything be more intolerable?

Some may draw comfort from the fact that Britain will be represented among the official controllers of the International Monetary Fund. Every one of the appointments of senior officials to the Federal Reserve Board was made by President Wilson, but that fact did not prevent it becoming the chosen weapon of Kuhn, Loeb and Company and their affiliated interests. So will it be with the new Fund. No power at present on earth (not even Dr. Dalton!) will be able to stop it carrying out the policy of the same group, again through the instrumentality of the Federal Reserve Board's overwhelming financial leverage.

By passing the Bretton Woods Bill, which it did without debate and in a hurried two hours, the British Labour majority made Great Britain a party to the creation of a World Bankers' State, armed with powers beyond anything hitherto enjoyed by men. Simultaneously it made Britain a party to her own ultimate destruction.

Comprehensive almost beyond belief as is the Bretton Woods enactment, it was still not considered sufficiently specific in its detail to guarantee the money-lenders against the continuance of British sovereignty, which after the defeat of Imperial Germany and of Tsarist Russia was given first priority for liquidation. When Paul Warburg announced after the First World War that other debtor countries might hope for leniency, he made the categorical assertion that Britain would be treated as a "case apart," and so, indeed, she was treated.

During the inter-war period the New York financial bosses waged incessant economic warfare against us. Its course during the first decade can be traced in a grimly interesting book "America Conquers Britain," by Ludwell Denny.

Our surrender of the command of the seas and our non-renewal of the Japanese Alliance have been noted. When we called upon America for a loan to fight the ravages of the depression the terms dictated were deliberately framed to create proletarian discontent and did in fact lead to the mutiny at Invergordon. After we had been forced out of the Wall Street orbit the attacks on us were redoubled and kept up until the outbreak of war, when the assault on our sovereign independence as a Great Power had to take second place to the more urgent assault on Hitler's Reich. But it was never abandoned, Reporting to the Legislative Assembly of the Province of Alberta in 1939, the Alberta Social Credit Board stated:

"The evidence is overwhelming that the objective of International Finance in the present struggle centred in the war is the destruction, for all practical purposes, of the British Commonwealth of Nations as the bulwark of democracy. There can be little doubt that the forces controlled by International Finance will be invoked to concentrate on the weakening of the sovereign power of the people, by means of a progressive centralisation of power. The rapid increase of the debt structure as a result of the war, the introduction of large-scale planning under bureaucratic central control, the impositions of harsh regulations and the rapid increase of taxation are methods which have already proved successful in consolidating financial control in the past under the pretext of war conditions. Therefore they are likely to be the methods used by International Finance at the present time in the pursuit of its objective of world domination . . ."

How lamentably true this prediction has been proved! Apart from its fulfilment inside Britain, the proofs of the prophesy lie in U.N.O., in Bretton Woods, and in the special measure drawn up to give Britain the coup de grace—the American Loan Agreement. Bretton Woods would have made any economic insulation of the British Empire a difficult and precarious undertaking: the Loan Agreement makes it an impossible one. It wipes out the sterling area and uses the euphemism "contraction" to define the abolition of Imperial Preference. Henceforward American goods and capital will sweep us from our Empire markets. The Federal Reserve Board will dictate our financial policy during the period of the loan-repayment, which means that it will enjoy a fifty years' usufruct of the Empire—or of what is now about to cease being the Empire.

Great Britain herself will be forced in repayment to sell more and more of her capital assets at home, as she has already sold them abroad. Unless a great upsurge of the national spirit moves her to a speedy revolt against these iniquities, she must become a mere financial colony—slum would be a more appropriate word—of Wall Street banksterdom.

An exaggeration? Perspicatious Americans do not think so. Said Mr. John Abbink, chairman of the National Foreign Trade Council of the U.S.:

"If the Bretton Woods plan and the U.S. loan to Britain are properly developed, the dollar will replace the pound as the monetary plan for world finance. The U.S. will become the greatest financial agent the world has ever known." For "U.S." read Wall Street and for "agent" read "master": the picture is then true. Mr. Abbink added: "The line of credit to be offered Britain, together with the settlement of Lend-Lease, is a small price to pay for the opportunity to plan a period of prosperity such as this country (the U.S.) has never known. I confess some doubt about the British ability to comply with all the conditions."

Unimaginable prosperity for America: Britain too impoverished to meet her commitments! President Truman contented himself with saying that the loan would be "good business" for America. Both the President and Mr. Abbink are greatly mistaken, however, if they suppose that there is any hope of permanent prosperity for America in this "good business," not only because of the flaw in the heart of the export capitalist system, but even more because permanent prosperity would ruin the entire money-lending racket. What *will* become permanent will be the stranglehold of the money-lenders over mankind.

There is, perhaps, a reservation to be made here. It may not be a stranglehold over the whole of mankind. Mr. Churchill in his Fulton speech referred to the shadow which has fallen over the Allied victory. There is some evidence that the same shadow has fallen over Wall Street. The modern international banking system —although its seed was sown in Britain by the financial advisers of William III, who in turn had imported it from Holland—did not begin to come into its own until the French Revolution had thoroughly watered the ground. The 1848 revolts strengthened its growth. Thereafter we find it developing in continuous association with the forces of the Left, whose Bolshevik revolution in 1917 it subsidized. Warburg and his friends nurtured the Russian Communist State with American money which they fed through German channels. Since then international capitalism and international socialism have planned many campaigns together; at this very time they are presenting a united front against Spain, Portugal and Argentina. Why this mutual attraction?

One reason, no doubt, is that the Money-Power possesses that which it may be expected to possess—money. And Communism has never shown that it despises money. Conversely, Bolshevism is a potent ally in undermining the Monarchial or National State, which is the only effective rival to the complete Bankers' State. Moreover, so long as the headquarters of the financial system are located in the most powerful industrial state, and so long as free enterprise therein is assured, the Money-Power in the ordinary course can have little objection to other nations establishing socialist economies.

Governments are peculiarly susceptible to the pressures which it knows so well how to exert: their contracts always go in largest measure to the entrenched vested interests. If every export and every import be made a Government contract, the Money-Power in the free enterprise country can look, therefore, to abundant profits and an absolute ultimate control. Potential rivals will also be eliminated—a first-class attraction. Mr. A. N. Field, who has done more than any man living to expose the wickedness of the financial system, summed up in these words the situation as it existed in 1932:

"The position is that international finance, by enticing the world into enormous debts and then withholding the means of payment, is

That position certainly existed fourteen years ago: it existed as recently as fourteen months ago. But now, as I say, has fallen the shadow. It is the not inconsiderable shadow of Russia.

Red Russia was the child of Wall Street finance, and even today she is not averse to borrowing from her parents, a well-known method of keeping affections sweet and fresh in that family relationship. Now, however, it has become exceedingly clear that such loans will be used for a purpose different from any thought possible before the war—the strengthening of Russia as an Imperialism which may rival and overthrow the Dollar Imperialism of the Federal Reserve Board. This does not mean that the quarrel is necessarily a permanent one: the tremendous anti-Russian "build-up" in America during the fortnight before Mr. Churchill's Fulton speech, for instance, may have been caused by some purely local dispute—such as the division of the spoils in Manchuria—and a permanent settlement may well see the two Imperialisms again at work breaking up and devouring the British Empire.

The quandary in which Britain finds herself is one of the utmost difficulty and menace. Any attempt to steer her own course by building up an Empire economy on a sane monetary basis would meet with immense opposition abroad, and be freely sabotaged at home by Fifth Columnists—both those serving Moscow and the others on the Right who seek to shelter behind the illusory aegis of America. There is, moreover, very little recognition in this country of the facts behind the conventional Press and B.B.C. facade.

Some men have fought bravely against Bretton Woods, it is true—at their head Messrs. Robert Boothby, Christopher Hollis, Norman Smith, Richard Stokes and Michael Foot in the House of Commons, Lord Beaverbrook and the Duke of Bedford in the House of Lords—

but as yet the picture of world affairs in their totality has been revealed to only a small fraction of the British people, and there is no doubt whatever that the ignorance of the rest has been deliberately fostered by the staging of political sham-fights for their distraction.

Unless enlightenment comes within the next few months Britain as a Great Power will cease to exist, and "sole sovereign sway and masterdom" over all British lands will pass into the keeping of a small group of master-usurers who know the value of everything in the world—providing it can be measured in terms of gold!

<u>Notes</u>

1. Doubt has since been cast on the authenticity of this quotation, but that it is in any case an authentic explanation of the aims and methods employed admits of no doubt[1].

2. Fifty years later this circular was declared to be a forgery, but nobody challenged it when Mr. Chas. A. Lindberg brought it to the notice of the House of Representatives in 1913. In any case, it describes precisely what did happen.

---

[1] Research is required to ascertain whether this quotation is correct. It is widely quoted on the internet with many writers giving the date as 1924 instead of 1934. Access to the original magazine is of course necessary.

About A.K. Chesterton

Arthur Kenneth Chesterton was born at the Luipaards Vlei gold mine, Krugersdorp, South Africa where his father was an official in 1899.

In 1915 unhappy at school in England A.K. returned to South Africa. There and without the knowledge of his parents, and having exaggerated his age by four years, he enlisted in the 5th South African Infantry.

Before his 17th birthday he had been in the thick of three battles in German East Africa. Later in the war he transferred as a commissioned officer to the Royal Fusiliers and served for the rest of the war on the Western Front being awarded the Military Cross in 1918 for conspicuous gallantry.

Between the wars A.K. first prospected for diamonds before becoming a journalist first in South Africa and then England. Alarmed at the economic chaos threatening Britain, he joined Sir Oswald Mosley in the B.U.F and became prominent in the movement. In 1938, he quarrelled with Mosley's policies and left the movement.

When the Second World War started he rejoined the army, volunteered for tropical service and went through all the hardships of the great push up from Kenya across the wilds of Jubaland through the desert of the Ogaden and into the remotest parts of Somalia. He was afterwards sent down the coast to join the Somaliland Camel Corps and intervene in the inter-tribal warfare among the Somalis.

In 1943 his health broke down and he was invalided out of the army with malaria and colitis, returning to journalism. In 1944, he became deputy editor and chief leader writer of *Truth*.

In the early 1950s A.K. established *Candour* and founded the League of Empire Loyalists which for some years made many colourful headlines in the press worldwide. He later took that organisation into The National Front, and served as its Chairman for a time.

A.K. Chesterton died in 1973.

A.K. Chesterton

About The A.K. Chesterton Trust

The A.K. Chesterton Trust was formed by Colin Todd and the late Miss. Rosine de Bounevialle in January 1996 to succeed and continue the work of the now defunct Candour Publishing Co.

The objects of the Trust are stated as follows:

"To promote and expound the principles of A.K. Chesterton which are defined as being to demonstrate the power of, and to combat the power of International Finance, and to promote the National Sovereignty of the British World."

Our aims include:

- *Maintaining and expanding the range of material relevant to A.K. Chesterton and his associates throughout his life.*

- *To preserve and keep in-print important works on British Nationalism in order to educate the current generation of our people.*

- *The maintenance and recovery of the sovereign independence of the British Peoples throughout the world.*

- *The strengthening of the spiritual and material bonds between the British Peoples throughout the world.*

- *The resurgence at home and abroad of the British spirit.*

We will raise funds by way of merchandising and donations.

We ask that our friends make provision for *The A.K. Chesterton Trust* in their will.

The A.K. Chesterton Trust has a **<u>duty</u>** to keep *Candour* in the ring and punching.

CANDOUR: To defend national sovereignty against the menace of international finance.

CANDOUR: To serve as a link between Britons all over the world in protest against the surrender of their world heritage.

<u>Subscribe to Candour</u>

CANDOUR SUBSCRIPTION RATES FOR 10 ISSUES.

U.K. £30.00
Europe 50 Euros.
Rest of the World £45.00.
USA $60.00.

All Airmail. Cheques and Postal Orders, £'s Sterling only, made payable to *The A.K. Chesterton Trust*. (Others, please send cash by **secure post**, $ bills or Euro notes.)

Payment by Paypal is available. Please see our website **www.candour.org.uk** for more information.

<u>Candour Back Issues</u>

Back issues are available. 1953 to the present.

Please request our back issue catalogue by sending your name and address with two 1st class stamps to:

The A.K. Chesterton Trust, BM Candour, London, WC1N 3XX, UK

Alternatively, see our website at **www.candour.org.uk** where you can order a growing selection on-line.

The A.K. Chesterton Trust Reprint Series

1. Creed of a Fascist Revolutionary & Why I Left Mosley - A.K. Chesterton.

2. The Menace of World Government & Britain's Graveyard - A.K. Chesterton.

3. What You Should Know About The United Nations - The League of Empire Loyalists.

4. The Menace of the Money-Power - A.K. Chesterton.

5. The Case for Economic Nationalism - John Tyndall.

6. Sound the Alarm! - A.K. Chesterton.

7. Six Principles of British Nationalism - John Tyndall.

8. B.B.C. - A National Menace - A.K. Chesterton.

9. Stand By The Empire - A.K. Chesterton.

10. Tomorrow. A Plan for the British Future - A.K. Chesterton.

Other Titles from The A.K. Chesterton Trust

Leopard Valley - A.K. Chesterton

Juma The Great - A.K. Chesterton

The New Unhappy Lords - A.K. Chesterton

Facing The Abyss - A.K. Chesterton

The History of the League of Empire Loyalists - McNeile & Black

All the above titles are available from The A.K. Chesterton Trust, BM Candour, London, WC1N 3XX, UK

www.candour.org.uk